To

ALWAYS KEEP IDEAS BREWING!!

"Laughing" Larry Beye

Instant Poetry
(Just Add Words!)

—— Third Edition ——

"Laughing" Larry Berger

iUniverse, Inc.
New York   Bloomington

Instant Poetry (Just Add Words!)

iUniverse books may be ordered through booksellers or by contacting:

iUniverse
1663 Liberty Drive
Bloomington, IN 47403
www.iuniverse.com
1-800-Authors (1-800-288-4677)

ISBN: 978-1-4502-5552-3 (pbk)
ISBN: 978-1-4502-5553-0 (ebk)

Printed in the United States of America

iUniverse rev. date: 9/28/10

Foreword

Greetings gentle reader:

Enclosed you will find several of Larry Burger's most
popular poems, as well as some of the lesser-known
ones. Originally written in 1999, this book has been
seen throughout the West Coast and has now entered its
third edition and become available around the globe. All
of the poems are in their original form, with no edits or
performance modifications. All were "written" onstage
between January and March of 1996 as part of APF
(audience participation free verse) sets at coffeehouses in
Los Angeles, California, where "Laughing" Larry Berger got
his start in poetry.

We sincerely hope you enjoy his work and, in reading this
poetry over and over, again a greater appreciation for it.

Thank you for your time!

The staff at Skysaje Enterprises

Contents

Bubble Gum 1

Leprosy..2

Catching Kumquats..3

Four Thousand Years Ago (The Crack Baby's Prayer)..................4

Green Tea Ice Cream 6

Exercising...7

Twenty Seconds to Midnight 8

Rock Star 9

Freedom 10

Reply for a Goddess..11

Yellow Velour Arm Chairs..12

Pooh 13

I Dropped My Four-Alarm Burrito..............................14

Vice, Christ, and Religion 15

A Woman's Fantasy 16

Ten-Foot Pole (for Brendan Constantine) 17

Escape of the Lost Angel (for G. C.) 18

Stop Laughing!..19

Ren and Stimpy 20

Gum Stuck on the Bottom of My Shoe 21

Wolverines 22

Frog Lips in Sulfuric Acid..23

GoastMowse (for D. B. G.)...24

Coin Clock..25

Diana's Dawn 26

Sunflower..28

I.D.G.F.F. 29

Donation$..31

Frog Town..33

The Ripples in My Flat Beer..34

Green Glinted Across His Glasses 35

Hats..37

Cold KFC in N.Y.C. 38

Bubble Gum

Soft and warm between my teeth,
an old lover returns
sweet and tangy inside my mouth.

Over and over she dances,
building evermore desire.

Slowly she turns up the heat,
stoking the fires
until
her passion's no longer confinable
She EXPLODES,
releasing the rapture of the moment!

And then
She slides along my tongue
For one
More
Tango

LEPROSY

Rotting corpses walking down the street
are they really so different from you and me?
They get up, go to work, come home,
all in steel and concrete coffins.

Much like the rest of us
Just plodding along
day after day after day.

Can some body tell me—
Honestly now—

What's the difference between a tomb and an apartment?

CATCHING KUMQUATS

Take your pick!
The farmer's market in Santa Monica
Or the night life on Hollywood Boulevard!

At either place you'll find them there.
Merchants selling strawberries by moonlight,
Occasionally handing out free samples,
Always begging for your business.

**CATCHING KUMQUATS AS THEY
STROLL BY**

FOUR THOUSAND YEARS AGO (THE CRACK BABY'S PRAYER)

Four thousand years ago,
The Nile ran red.
Red with the blood of a people yearning for freedom.

Five hundred years ago,
The Hudson ran red,
Red with the blood of a people losing their homes and lives
to the new kids on the block.

Fifty years ago,
Los Angeles burned,
Burned with the fires of injustice
Built up over generations.

Twenty years ago
Los Angeles burned again,
This time with the fires
Forged of broken promises
And dashed hopes.

This morning I was born—
Born with an addiction not my own,
Born with nothing
But the chance to die
And the hope that it will happen soon.

Four thousand years ago,
the Nile ran red.

What color will the rivers run for me?

Green Tea Ice Cream

Things are good;
life is going smoothly;
summer is almost here.

Three years is a long time,
but not when you need to prepare
for disasters of biblical proportions

The psychics say the world will end in 2012,
suns have gone nova, and we're all going to die.

Right now
I've got my green tea ice cream.
I'm happy.

Exercising

I hate going to the gym!
All those people
watching my every move,
thinking how mine compares to their own bodies.

I'm not into working out at home either.
I get bored on the treadmill.
Running and running and getting nowhere.
It reminds me too much of life.

Just give me a nice walk
on a starry night
or just before dawn on the street
with the cars going by.

Some call it meditation;
I call it exercise!

Twenty Seconds to Midnight

It's not enough time!
Quick, somebody hand me the knife!
The ball is falling!
Champagne is flowing!
Blood is drip-ping from my pen!

Please, Lord God, help me
There is just not enough time!
How can you write anything decent
in just twenty seconds!

Rock Star

Dawn comes to the
Red mountain temple.

Pure and golden,
warm goodness filled with light.

"But it's only a paper moon."
A woman dressed in red starts to sing
She is very much off-key

Sleeping on the bus has made people cranky.
They start yelling for the driver to put her off the bus at the
next stop.

I say cut her some slack!
Maybe nobody told her we'd be up so high.
Some people just shouldn't travel above 5,000 feet.

Freedom

Your eagle's wings carry me away.
Love and glory mean nothing without you.
You are the goddess to which we pray as we earn our daily
bread

Reply for a Goddess

You offer me a treasure
far beyond the dreams
of mortal men.
Just
one
single
night with you
could satisfy the eternal lust
of Zeus himself!
But alas,
I am only a man
with naught but human emotions,
Frailties,
and I could never possibly worship you
As you truly deserve.
For I am but a mere mortal,
And I have no powers to grant
All I would ever possibly have
to offer you would be my heart!
Ah, but then again—
Tell me please,
How can I possibly give you
That which you already own?

Yellow Velour Arm Chairs

During the days of King Arthur,
the gentry were regarded as noble.
Gallant knights in shining armor,
ladies at court with gowns flowing.

Valiant warriors
trying to win the hand of a fair maiden
would battle in tournaments for their favor
as the ladies watched from bronze thrones.

In modern times, little has changed.
Oh sure, now ladies have joined the games,
And today's warriors use blades forged of ideas,
And words craft their armor in place of iron, but the battles
rage on.

In the days of the round table, the gentry seated themselves
on bronze thrones. In modern times, our noble word warriors
seat themselves on
Yellow velour arm chairs.

Pooh

"Hurry, Piglet! We need to set the table! Christopher Robin
will be here any minute!
Honey! We need more honey!"

Think think
Think think
Think think

Christopher Robin is in his forties now.
His kids can't stand him, and his wife is filing for divorce.

He picks up the dry cleaning for the last time; he starts to
wonder, "Where is Pooh now that I really need him?"

Think think
Think think
Think think

I Dropped My Four-Alarm Burrito

There's no need for waterworks!
I'll go out in a blaze of glory!
But the fire department
Doesn't always go to Mexico.
After all, this is LA,
And a run for the border
Doesn't always mean the same thing.

Vice, Christ, and Religion

Services begin on Monday night
at precisely 6:47 PM.

I have cleansed myself
from the cares of the day,
dressed in ritual garb,
And I have removed my shoes
For I will be treading upon sacred ground.

God has come home.
A flick of the finger opens the universe.

His Christ, too, is truly magnificent:
56 incredible inches and fully interactive!

Hour upon hour I prostrate myself before their altar. To
my right are additional offerings of the sacred beverage—
premium draft style of course—
And stacked neatly in rows of six by six.

To my left are offerings of the cleansing food,
The holy popcorn and potato chips.

In my right hand I hold the conduit
For divine inspiration.
I have achieved nirvana!
I am Complete.

A Woman's Fantasy

"Once, just once,
I wish he'd turn off that damned TV
And take me out for dinner!

It wouldn't have to be anything fancy.
Hell, I'd settle for a two-for-one night at Pizza Hut!

It was different when we were dating.
He was captain of the football team,
And we were so in love!

We used to hang out at the malt shop all the time!
Talking, eating hot fudge sundaes, dreaming about the future.
I even gave him my cherry!
But now after some twenty years with him I find myself
asking

WHY??????????????????????????"

Ten-Foot Pole
(for Brendan Constantine)

What ever happened to Lech Walesa?
Clinton? Gore-Bitch-Off? Ray-gun?
They all lied to us, man!
There's no new world order!
Democratic Communism didn't work
And America is paying the price!

Thousands homeless
or out of work, downing
Anti-depressant medication
As that statue out in the harbor
Spreads her legs to the world.

The shrinks tell me that
I'll fly north or south with the wind,
And here I sit stuck somewhere in the middle

Impaled on a ten-foot Pole named Irving
And NOBODY, DAMN IT, NOBODY PLAYS
MOZART ANYMORE!!!!!!!!!!!!!!!!!!!!!!!!!!!!

Escape of the Lost Angel
(for G. C.)

Rising
Like the phoenix
from the cleansing flames.

Demon hands clawing at the purest spirit
to snuff out the light.

He who summons tries in vain,
And the lost angel wings his way home.

A chain forged of blood
wraps itself around his skull.

A last-ditch effort to keep his spirit bound;
yet, down though the centuries, it is his will that has
been strengthened.

The horns fall away,
And the lost angel wings his way home.

Stop Laughing!

Why?
What's wrong
with having a highly developed sense of humor?
Laughter is the wave of joy and nature's first breath!

To stop laughing
is to resign ourselves to
coffins of skin!

To have eyes vacant of life
Stare back from our reflections
in the mirror.

Stop laughing?

Somehow

I don't think so!!!

Ren and Stimpy

Time and chaos personified.
The spokesperson for the modern generation.
"You Idiot!!!"
They say that God is a fool,
So why not animate him?

Gum Stuck on the Bottom of My Shoe

"Scrape 'em off!"
That's what my mother always used to say.
"You don't need dem gold-digging whores!!!"

"But, if you should find a voman to love you,
To bare your children, zuch a thing vould be verth all da money in da verld!"

When I turned eighteen my father pulled me
Aside and gave me this advice: "Zon," he says to me, "You and I have been listening to your mother's advice for most of your life. Look at vere it's gotten me.

"I'm eating baby food three months out of the year because of digestion troubles, and I've been drunk more than I've been zober.

"Ven I vas your hage,
My pa pulled me aside and told me that you've vgot to go through three tons of shit just to find von diamond, and I thought I'd found one when I married your mom, but look at me! I ain't made more than $20,000 a year, and all I've got left to hope for is to help you avoid the same mistakes!!!"
I'm still not sure who was right, but I'm still looking for that diamond girl, so I'm begging please
Somebody hand me a shovel!

Wolverines

Comic books and candy bars,
Claws that can tear through memories—
A warrior's blood quickens the chase.

A woman with red hair smiles
from across the room.
Power falls from his eyes
as she dances with someone else.

Perhaps someone can help me.
Even with the healing factor,
Is adamantium strong enough
To mend a broken heart?

Frog Lips in Sulfuric Acid

PRINCE CHARMING DOESN'T
LIVE HERE ANY MORE!

After that cop broke my bottle of love potion #9 back in the
day, I went back to that old gypsy bitch, stuck my size 15s in
her face a few times, and smashed that crystal ball upside her
head till the bitch gave me a refund!

Kiss this frog
and his lips don't spew
nothing but sulfuric acid!

It'll burn the stardust out of your eyes
and rip your mask away,
force you to take a good look
at who you really are,
maybe for the first time in your life!

so you'd best ask yourself :
do you really want to take the risk,
Or do you just want to spend the night?

GoastMowse
(for D. B. G.)

Home at last with my muse
to channel the words into song!

She always knows what file to open
To touch a little spot in my heart!

She's a crafty little devil!
Always changing shape, form, and function.
Occasionally, we fall into sync and find the cheese together,
for in my virtual palace, it helps to have a tour=guide through
the maze!

I love my little GoastMowse
but she kind pisses off my wife though.
She gets jealous because they both have to
Vie for my attention.

But truth be told, my wife really loves the GoastMowse, too.

After all, she can't spell worth a darn either and clicking icons
is much easier than those damned arrow keys!

Coin Clock

The Chromos currency exchange
just opened a branch office
in my neighborhood.

Time for ca$h,
the old dance continues;
only the I.R.S. reaps the benefits.

They deal mainly in personal loans
With terms averaging seventy years or so.
When it's over
You die.

Diana's Dawn

History records not accurately the fall of Olympus. Yet if you were to search the records the truth may be found.

For 'twas to be the hour of victory for the Titans!
Lord Chronos had dealt his son Zeus a mortal blow. Cerberus had been called from Hades to serve his true master and held Apollo at bay.

There was, however, one more warrior present, though as a mere goddess she was considered insignificant and, well, just plain not worth the bother.

Yet, Diana was free to act, and so act she did.
Arching her bow to form the crescent moon, she sent a message arrow into the great ocean requesting his aid. Now as it happened the, arrow struck ocean full in the chest and distracted him long enough for Poseidon to win the battle for the sea, but that is a tale for another time. Upon reading the message, Poseidon granted her request and parted the waters of the great sea and called forth warriors from the world of men!

Now these warriors came fully equipped for battle, but not with blades or bows or armor or shields or other accoutrements fit for battle in the world of men. No, they came fit for battle with the gods themselves, for they came armed with brush and with quill! With ink and vellum! With the music of the lyre and all the colors of the rainbow!

With these they captured the God of time and forced him back, back into the blow meant for his son!

Zeus then cast his bolt, opening Tartarus and carrying the day.

Now, ever since, these warriors have been mistakenly dubbed the children of Apollo.

For in the end, 'twas his rays which brought Cerberus to heel and gave the warriors
Their opening.

However, as the Gods drank their first cup of Ambrosia the next bright morn, Zeus himself
Heralded the bright new day, as Diana's Dawn!

Sunflower

Touched by the Gods
She carries her obsession,
Following the sunrise
With the fruits of her tears.

Throughout eternity
She follows her heart's desire,
Mourning her lover through the darkness
Until he returns at dawn.

And her name is Sunflower

I.D.G.F.F.

"What are you afraid of?"
"Would it really be that bad to have even just one person you
can come home to? That you can talk to about anything?"

YES!

The last time brought us to the edge of the grave,
With me leading the way, and I'm not about to let that happen
again!

The blackness,
The eternal dark of oblivion would be far sweeter than living
with the knowledge that helping me deal with my pain caused
yours.

"What's the worst that could happen?"

Surgery pulls me back from the edge of the abyss
after removing the blade from my heart.

Blood flows in a red river
washing me clean,
not to escape from your love,
but because I DO give a damn
and I care too much about you
To force you to lower yourself and
Hang out with a no good bum like me!

I'm just plain not worth it!
I'd much rather die than let you get
close.

The key to the door is
the eight-inch chef's knife
with the pearl handle.

The door is open!
I'm coming home!

Donation$

Excuse me, sir.
My name is
Lawrence Richard Berger
And I am a proponent of
reverse pan-handling.

Would you like some change?
No really! Would you?

You see,
as I'm walking down the street
on my way to the bus stop,
I often see the same three people.

It never fails!
They are there most every single day.

The first one has a chain around his neck,
held there not with a lock, but with a banjo.

The second is a man of color.
 Not black, but silver from head to toe!
I found out his name was Tron.

The third guy just
had his legs blown off in the war.
All of them have cups in their hands,
Begging for change.

Living in the area
has taught me that it's
really money they are after.

They count on the fact that
People will throw coins
In the cups as if to say:

"Here!
Take my money and go away!
Hit the snooze bar!
I don't need your wake-up call!"

Well, like I said, I've lived in the area.
They know that as a poet
I don't have a lot of money.

All I can offer them is change.

Frog Town

Dreams are the
downward staircases
into the realms of reality.

They are the subconscious insects,
buzzing their way through the void
to create our world.

Frogs are famous for eating insects,
and Frog Town is their domain.

Frogs and insects depend on each other.
Insects depend on frogs to keep them
Sharp and alert.

Frogs depend on insects to
satisfy their greed.

Frog town is Hollywood,
and frog town can be
a heavenly place for
an insect!

Well, At least till suppertime anyway.

The Ripples in My Flat Beer

It's begun.
There is no stopping it now.
Somewhere somebody dropped
the pebble, and no old lady
can bring it back from the sea.

So what do you do?
What do you do after
the children have grown
and you come home to find
your wife crying?

What do you do
When you lose your job?
Your company goes bankrupt?
Your stocks have crashed?

Tell me what do you do?
What do you do?
What do you do?
Tell me please:
just how do I escape
from the ripples in my flat beer?

Green Glinted Across His Glasses

Green glinted across his glasses;
she just could not resist.

Forgetting the vows
She had taken,
She let her passions rule the moment.

And then the alarm clock rings,
bringing with it the dawn of a new day.

A day where she fumbles for the controls
To the hydraulic bed
To lower her into the wheelchair, which she
pushes with all the power in her soul.

As her two moveable fingers
press her way to the door,
the thought occurs to her that
her aide is on time for a change.

It has to be her aide
No one else comes to visit her
since that hussy took over.

The door opens inward;
It's the aide.
The aide says:
"My you look pretty
Today, Reverend Mother!"

The comment puts the twinkle
back in her eyes.

For at 83
And a stroke victim,
She still remembers that
Green glinted across his glasses.

Hats

We all wear them,
No matter what our eyes say.
We are Father, Child, Mother,
Doctor, Lawyer, Friend, Councilor,
Lover, Soldier, Etc., Etc., Etc.

But who cries for the children
who are natural-born millionaires
in the making?

And why do we spend
so much time killing
their dreams?

Cold KFC in N.Y.C.

As I'm riding home on the B.T.A.,
it suddenly hits me that things could have gone a hell of a lot
worse.

You see,
an hour ago
I was kissing concrete
back at Grand Central
with the barrel of a
.357 shoved into the back
Of my skull.

"You never saw my face!" The guy screams.
"Keep your eyes on the ground!"

After a while, I hear his footfalls,
so I stand up, and at my feet I
find my wallet, with twenty dollars
more in it than I thought I'd have.

A beer- and yearn-soaked wino
just sat down next to me. The stench is
almost overpowering! But I've got to tell
you, no rose ever smelled sweeter!

Snow crunches under my feet as
I climb out of the subway and head for home. Terminal Island,
with its high-rise buildings and high-rise bank accounts, seems
a universe away from the vagrants warming their hands over
burning trash cans filled with rotting fish heads

And dog shit.

They pass 40-ounce bottles and swap stories like the bards of
ancient Viking legends as I pass by.

My flat doesn't have any heat,
only an old pot-bellied stove,
The kitchenette, and a mattress where I collapse
From exhaustion. No mansion was ever grander!

Hours later, I wake hungry.
There is nothing to eat in the fridge
Except some cold KFC leftovers.

And folks,
I've got to tell you:
ROADKILL NEVER TASTED SO GOOD!

And with that, gentle reader, we come to the close of this book. I hope you have enjoyed reading these poems as much as I did writing them—and please contact me with your comments!

To contact "Laughing" Larry Berger, here is the address info:

Skysaje Enterprises
50 Amesbury Rd.
Rochester, NY 14623

laughingl@yahoo.com

(585)334-6388